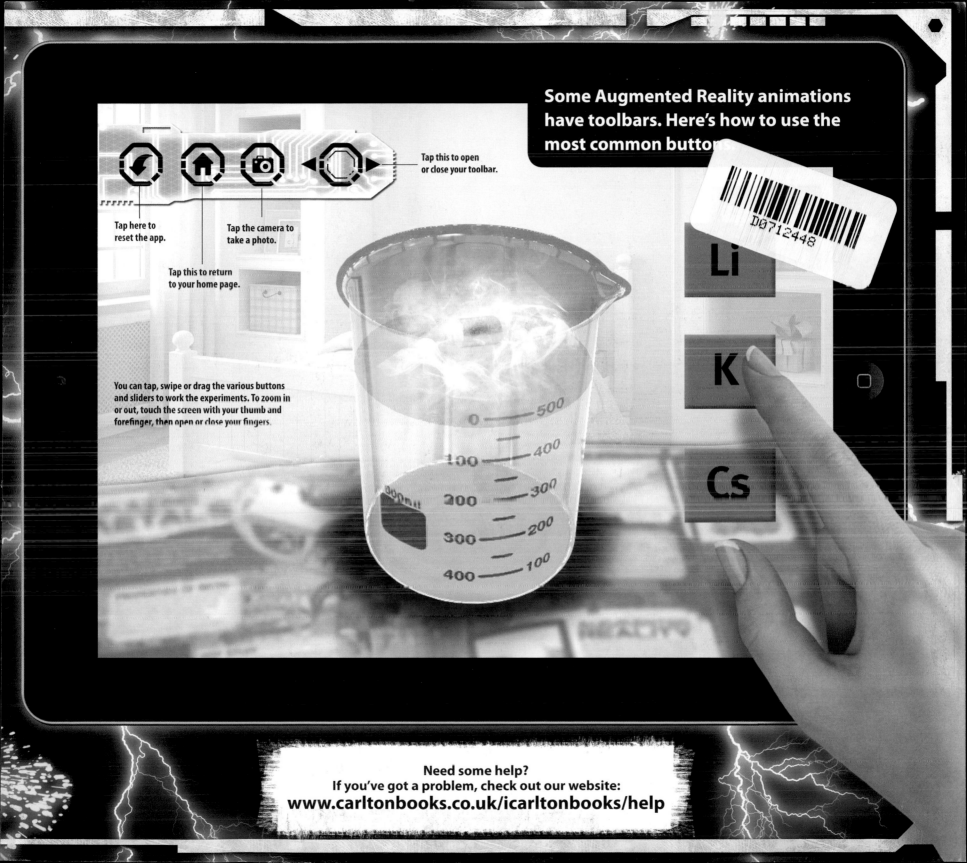

Some Augmented Reality animations have toolbars. Here's how to use the most common buttons.

Tap this to open or close your toolbar.

Tap here to reset the app.

Tap the camera to take a photo.

Tap this to return to your home page.

You can tap, swipe or drag the various buttons and sliders to work the experiments. To zoom in or out, touch the screen with your thumb and forefinger, then open or close your fingers.

Need some help?
If you've got a problem, check out our website:
www.carltonbooks.co.uk/icarltonbooks/help

CAUTION! EXPLOSIVE SCIENCE!

CARLTON
KiDS

THIS IS A CARLTON BOOK

Text, design and illustration © Carlton Books Limited 2015
Published in 2015 by Carlton Books Limited,
An imprint of the Carlton Publishing Group,
20 Mortimer Street, London, W1T 3JW.

A catalogue record for this book is available from
the British Library.

ISBN: 978-1-78312-098-7
Printed in Dongguan, China.

Consultants: Anne Rooney
                 Jack Challoner
Executive Editor: Selina Wood
Design Director: Russell Porter
Design: Jake da'Costa, Mark Walker
Augmented Reality: Alessandro Mondaini
Picture Research: Paul Langan
Production: Charlotte Cade
Publisher: Russell McLean

Picture Credits
The publishers would like to thank the following sources for their kind permission
to reproduce the pictures in this book.

Key: t = top, b = bottom, l = left, r = right & c = centre

7t Corbis/Jerome Favre/epa, 7r Shutterstcock, 7br Getty Images/Peter Essick/Aurora, 8bl & 8c,
9t Shutterstock, 9br Getty Images/Moment, 10bl Getty Images/Bill Pugliano, 10br, 10-11
Shutterstock, 11l Getty Images/Ryan Pierse, 11t Science Photo Library/NREL/US Department
of Energy, 11cl, 11tr Shutterstock, 11br Getty Images/Henrik Sorensen/Stone, 12bl Science
Photo Library/David Ducros, 12-13, 13br Shutterstock, 13t Science Photo Library, 14bl, 14c,
Shutterstock, 14-15 Getty Images/Al Bello, 15tr Shutterstock, 15br preschoolpowolpackets.
blogspot.co.uk, 15l Science Photo Library/Trevor Clifford Photography, 16bl Corbis/Ron Sachs/
CNP, 16-17 Getty Images/E+, 17t Science Photo Library/Charles D. Winters, 17r (x4), 17bc
Shutterstock, 18bl Science Photo Library/Photostock Israel, 18 Getty Images/Ezra Shaw, 18-19
Titelist, 19br Shutterstock, 19c Getty Images/The Image Bank, 19tr Alamy/EPA, 20l Science
Photo Library/Frans Lanting, 20r Thinkstock, 20-21 Alamy, 21t Getty Images/Paul Crock/AFP,
21b, 22b Science Photo Library/Ria Novosti, 22-23 Getty Images, 23 Getty Images/Franck Fife/
AFP, 23r Science Photo Library/Tony MccConnell, 23br Science Photo Library/Gustoimages,
24b Getty Images/Photographer's Gallery, 24-25 Shutterstock, 25tr Science Photo Library/
Erich Schrempp, 25c Getty Images, 25b Corbis/Radius Images, 26bl Shutterstock, 26t Getty
Images/The Image Bank, 26b Science Photo Library/U.S. Department of Defense, 26-27, 27r
Shutterstock, 27t Science Photo Library/ESA, 27b Science Photo Library/Jonathan Watts,
28bl Science Photo Library/Ted Kinsman, 28r, 28-29, 29l 29t Shuttertock, 29tr Science Photo
Library/Martyn F. Chillmaid, 29br Corbis/TEK Image/Science Photo Library, 30c Getty Images,
30bl, 30-31, 31tr Shutterstock, 31l Science Photo Library/Los Alamos National Laboratory

iSCIENCE

CLIVE GIFFORD

ASTONISHING ATOMS

Atoms are tiny particles that form the building blocks of all matter in the Universe. How tiny? Well, a single human hair is around 300,000 atoms wide. The word "atom" comes from the ancient Greek, "atmos", meaning indivisible. We now know that atoms can be broken down into smaller parts, called subatomic particles.

Electron

Neutrons

Protons

INSIDE AN ATOM

An atom is made up mostly of empty space, but at its centre is a nucleus containing particles with a positive electrical charge known as protons. The nucleus often has an equal number of particles with no charge, called neutrons. Outside the nucleus are smaller particles called electrons. These carry a negative electrical charge.

Protons   Neutrons   Electrons

An oxygen atom (main picture) has 8 protons, 8 neutrons and 8 electrons. Atoms usually have the same number of electrons as protons, so the electric charges balance out.

ATOMIC NUMBER

When an element is listed on the Periodic Table (see next page), it has two numbers. The smaller number is its atomic number – the number of protons in the nucleus of each of its atoms. The larger number is the mass number – the total number of neutrons and protons in the nucleus. An atom of silicon has 14 protons and 14 neutrons. It has an atomic mass of 28. Hydrogen is unique – it has no neutron in its nucleus, just one proton, so its atomic and mass numbers are both 1.

atomic number

14

Si

Silicon

28

mass number

ISOTOPES

Isotopes are the atoms of elements that have a different number of neutrons. Carbon atoms normally have 12 neutrons but carbon-14 has two extra. Carbon-14 is found in all living things and changes to carbon-12 at a known rate (by losing its two extra neutrons). After about 5,730 years, for instance, only half the original carbon-14 remains. Scientists measure the amount of carbon-14 in ancient animal and plant remains to estimate their age.

Scientists used carbon dating to determine that this baby mammoth, Lyuba, discovered in Arctic Russia in 2007, is about 42,000 years old.

ATOMS FUSING

In nuclear fusion, the nuclei of atoms fuse, joining together to form heavier particles and generating energy. Nuclear fusion occurs in the cores of stars such as the Sun. There, under intense pressure and temperatures as high as 15 million ºC, the nuclei of hydrogen atoms fuse, forming helium gas and releasing vast amounts of energy.

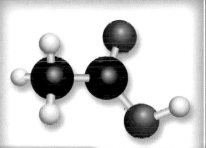

Electron

A molecule of acetic acid contains 4 hydrogen (white), 2 carbon (black) and 2 oxygen (red) atoms. Acetic acid is the main component of vinegar.

MOLECULE MATTERS

Atoms can join together to form molecules. Some molecules are made up of the same type of atom. Ozone, for example, consists of three oxygen atoms and is named by scientists as O_3. Other molecules are made up of different types of atoms. A molecule of glucose, a type of sugar, contains 12 hydrogen atoms, six carbon and six oxygen atoms.

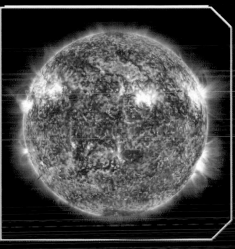

➤The Sun fuses around 620 million metric tons of hydrogen each second, generating heat and light energy that pours out into space.

AUGMENTED REALITY

Explore the structures of hydrogen, lithium, carbon, oxygen and caesium atoms. Then press the button to split the uranium-235 atom.

NUCLEAR FISSION

Nuclear fission occurs when the nucleus of an atom is split, releasing neutrons and energy. The free neutrons hit the nuclei of other atoms, making them split as well and causing a chain reaction that generates phenomenal energy. One kilogram of uranium-235 fuel used in nuclear power stations produces as much energy as 1,500,000kg of coal.

Nuclear fission takes place inside the reactor of a nuclear power station. The energy heats water into steam which drives turbines to generate electricity.

AWESOME ELEMENTS

Everything that exists, from a planet or an aeroplane to this book, is made up of elements. An element is matter that only contains one type of atom – such as iron, carbon, hydrogen or sulphur. Elements cannot be broken down into simpler substances. Instead, they form the building blocks of everything around you – as well as you!

COMMON OR RARE?

The most common element in the Universe is hydrogen. Hydrogen is the simplest element and all other elements are made from it. Oxygen makes up almost half of the Earth's crust. In contrast, the element astatine is rare. Less than 30g of it is believed to exist on Earth at any one time.

Some elements appear in different forms. Carbon exists as coal (above), graphite (the "lead" in pencils) and diamond.

MIXTURES

Mixtures are two or more different elements that have been physically mixed together. Sand in water, milk, fog and the collection of nitrogen, oxygen, argon and other gases in air, are all physical mixtures.

You can easily see that this breakfast cereal is a mixture of flakes and berries — but in chemical mixtures the particles are too small to see.

GROUP 1

1 H Hydrogen

3 Li Lithium 7	4 Be Beryllium 9
11 Na Sodium 23	12 Mg Magnesium 24
19 K Potassium 39	20 Ca Calcium 40

21 Sc Scandium 45	22 Ti Titanium 48	23 V Vanadium 51	24 Cr Chromium 52	25 Mn Manganese 55
39 Y Yttrium 89	40 Zr Zirconium 91	41 Nb Niobium 93	42 Mo Molybdenum 96	43 Tc Technetium 98
72 Hf Hafnium 178	73 Ta Tantalum 181	74 W Tungsten 184	75 Re Rhenium 186
104 Rf Rutherfordium 261	105 Db Dubnium 262	106 Sg Seaborgium 263	107 Bh Bohrium 264

37 Rb Rubidium 85	38 Sr Strontium 88
55 Cs Caesium 133	56 Ba Barium 137
87 Fr Francium 223	88 Ra Radium 226

57 La Lanthanum 139	58 Ce Cerium 140	59 Pr Praseodymium 141	60 Nd Neodymium 144
89 Ac Actinium 227	90 Th Thorium 232	91 Pa Protactinium 231	92 U Uranium 238

Alkali Metals
Alkaline Earth Metals
Transition Metals
Post-Transition Metals
Metalloids
Other Non-Metals
Halogens
Noble Gases
Lanthanoids
Actinoids
Transuranium Elements

COMPOUNDS

When elements chemically react and make bonds with other elements, they form compounds. Silicon and oxygen bond together in compounds that make up sand and rocks. Many compounds have quite different properties from the elements they are made from. Chlorine (a poisonous gas) and sodium (a reactive metal) can bond to form a compound you eat – sodium chloride, or table salt.

Salt (sodium chloride, written as NaCl), contains equal amounts of sodium and chlorine.

THE PERIODIC TABLE

The first attempt to draw up a table of elements was made by Russian scientist, Dmitri Mendeleev, in 1869. The modern Periodic Table contains over 90 elements found in nature, plus a number of elements that have been made in laboratories by scientists. The latest named are livermorium and flerovium (2012).

Each element has a symbol, often made up of the first two letters of the element's name.

GROUP 18

TABLE TALK

The Periodic Table arranges elements in horizontal rows called periods. As we move across the table from left to right in a period, the number of electrons in an atom increases one at a time. The vertical columns of the table are called groups. All elements in a group tend to share chemical and physical characteristics. For example, Group 1 are the Alkali metals which react with lots of other elements while Group 18 are the Noble gases. These have no smell or colour and do not react with other elements.

5 B Boron 11	6 C Carbon 12	7 N Nitrogen 14	8 O Oxygen 16	9 F Fluorine 19	2 He Helium 4
13 Al Aluminium 27	14 Si Silicon 28	15 P Phosphorus 31	16 S Sulphur 32	17 Cl Chlorine 35	10 Ne Neon 20
					18 Ar Argon 40

26 Fe Iron 56	27 Co Cobalt 59	28 Ni Nickel 59	29 Cu Copper 63	30 Zn Zinc 65	31 Ga Gallium 70	32 Ge Germanium 73	33 As Arsenic 75	34 Se Selenium 79	35 Br Bromine 80	36 Kr Krypton 84
44 Ru Ruthenium 101	45 Rh Rhodium 102	46 Pd Palladium 106	47 Ag Silver 108	48 Cd Cadmium 112	49 In Indium 115	50 Sn Tin 119	51 Sb Antimony 122	52 Te Tellurium 128	53 I Iodine 127	54 Xe Xenon 131
76 Os Osmium 190	77 Ir Iridium 192	78 Pt Platinum 195	79 Au Gold 197	80 Hg Mercury 201	81 Tl Thallium 205	82 Pb Lead 207	83 Bi Bismuth 209	84 Po Polonium 209	85 At Astatine 210	86 Rn Radon 222
108 Hs Hassium 265	109 Mt Meitnerium 268	110 Ds Darmstadtium 281	111 Rg Roentgenium 273	112 Cn Copernicium 285	113 Uut Ununtrium 284	114 Fl Flerovium 289	115 Uup Ununpentium 288	116 Lv Livermorium 293	117 Uus Ununseptium 292	118 Uuo Ununoctium 294

| 61 Pm Promethium 145 | 62 Sm Samarium 150 | 63 Eu Europium 152 | 64 Gd Gadolinium 157 | 65 Tb Terbium 159 | 66 Dy Dysprosium 163 | 67 Ho Holmium 165 | 68 Er Erbium 167 | 69 Tm Thulium 169 | 70 Yb Ytterbium 173 | 71 Lu Lutetium 175 |
| 93 Np Neptunium 237 | 94 Pu Plutonium 244 | 95 Am Americium 243 | 96 Cm Curium 247 | 97 Bk Berkelium 247 | 98 Cf Californium 251 | 99 Es Einsteinium 252 | 100 Fm Fermium 257 | 101 Md Mendelevium 258 | 102 No Nobelium 259 | 103 Lr Lawrencium 262 |

Noble gases have lots of uses. Helium, which is lighter than air, is used to fill balloons, while neon is found in colourful lighting.

THE MATERIAL WORLD

The Helix Bridge pedestrian bridge in Singapore is made of the metal stainless steel, which is strong and does not rust easily.

All things possess a large range of characteristics, or properties, such as colour, weight and strength, or the ability to absorb water or be waterproof. Understanding the properties of materials allows designers, engineers and craftsmen to select and use the right material for a particular job.

HARDNESS AND STRENGTH

Hardness is how resistant a material is to being scratched or shaped. The Mohs Scale is a measure of the hardness of rocks and minerals. The soft mineral talc is at one end of the scale and extremely hard diamonds are at the other. Strength is the ability of a material to carry a load or bear stress. The maximum stress a material can bear before it breaks or fails is called its tensile strength.

HEATING UP

All materials have a melting point (the point at which they turn from a solid to a liquid) and a boiling point (the temperature at which they turn from a liquid to a gas). Gallium, for instance, is a solid metal at room temperature but has a melting point of just under 30°C – if you held it in hands it would melt.

If a material is a good thermal conductor, as many metals are, heat passes through it easily. Thermal insulators, such as plastic, resist the flow of heat.

Firefighters' protective clothing includes materials like Nomex which is fire-resistant and does not let heat pass through easily.

In a car crash test, the strong but easy-to-shape steel of the car's body crumples but the brittle glass windscreen shatters.

DID YOU KNOW?

Aerogels are solid materials that are incredibly light but strong – some can support more than 1,000 times their own weight without breaking. Aerogels are also thermal insulators. A silica aerogel tile placed over a flame will only melt if the flame reaches 1,200°C.

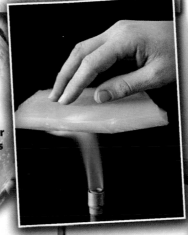

STATES OF MATTER

All materials are found in one of three states: solid, liquid or gas. The particles in a solid are tightly packed together and take up a definite space. The particles in a liquid are close together but can slide past one another so that a liquid can flow to take up the shape of a container it is in. In a gas, the particles are spaced further apart in no regular pattern. Gases naturally fill any container they are put into, instantly spreading out. They can also be compressed (squashed) easily.

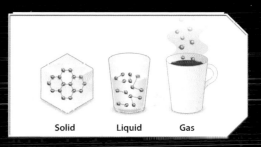

Solid   Liquid   Gas

FLEXIBILITY

When you ping a rubber band, you are demonstrating the property of elasticity – the ability of some flexible materials to return to their original shape after being stretched or bent. A vaulter's pole, made of fibreglass and carbon fibres, Is extremely elastic, almost bending in two. Materials with great plasticity, such as clay, can be shaped or deformed and stay in this new shape permanently.

After bending, a vaulter's pole springs back into shape and propels the athlete over the bar.

CHANGES OF STATE

Matter will change state if it is heated or cooled because this increases or decreases the energy of the particles that make up the matter. A heated solid may melt, turning into a liquid. A heated liquid may evaporate, turning into a gas. A cooled gas will condense to a liquid and a cooled liquid will freeze to a solid. Some solids can change into a gas without passing through a liquid phase. This is called sublimation. Dry ice is a solid form of carbon dioxide. When placed at room temperature, it changes into a gas.

⌐ The smoky gas created by dry ice is used at concerts and in movies as a special effect.

AUGMENTED REALITY

Now you can experiment with the solid, liquid and gas forms of water (H_2O). Heat up some ice and see it melt into water. Then heat the water up to the correct temperature to create steam!

AMAZING METALS

From aluminium to zinc and many more in-between, metals make up more than three quarters of all the elements found in the Universe. Only one metal, mercury, is a liquid at room temperature. The rest are solids and, apart from copper and gold, have a grey or silver appearance.

PROPERTIES OF METAL

Most metals are hard, tough and strong. Many can also be drawn into wires or beaten and shaped into panels. These properties make metals incredibly useful materials for construction, and for making tools and machines such as computers, cars and planes.

HOT STUFF

Heat flows through metals readily, making metal a good material for saucepans, cooking utensils and heating elements. The particles in metals are held together by strong bonds which means it takes a lot of energy to separate them. As a result, many metals have high melting points. Aluminium's melting point is 660°C, copper's is 1,085°C while titanium melts at 1,668°C.

Steel is a metal alloy made from iron mixed with other metals and carbon. Steel makes up around 60—70 per cent of a typical car's weight.

Molybdenum has a very high melting point of 2,623ºC. Mixed with other materials, it's used in the heat shields of spacecraft to stop them burning up as they re-enter Earth's atmosphere.

LIGHT AND HEAVY

Lithium is the least dense metal ($0.54g$ per cm^3) while osmium is the most dense at $22.6g$ per cm^3 – that's twice as heavy as lead and over 20 times heavier than water. A paper bag full of osmium would weigh as much as a motor car!

Osmium is the heaviest metal of all.

MINING METALS

Many metals are found in Earth's crust in rocky ores and people have developed different industrial processes to extract them. Iron is extracted from ore called haematite by heating it in a blast furnace, while electricity is used to remove aluminium from bauxite.

⌐Copper is often used for making pipes because it doesn't react with water.

As gold doesn't corrode, it's often used in jewellery and other treasures, such as Tutankhamun's mask.

DO THEY REACT?

Some metals, like gold and platinum, are largely unreactive. Metals that don't react with many common substances such as water or air, have many uses in industry. Other metals, though, are highly reactive. Alkali metals such as sodium, lithium, caesium and potassium can pop, fizz and even explode in chemical reactions.

MAGNETIC METALS

Some metals, such as iron, nickel and cobalt are magnetic. This means they are attracted by the force of magnetism. Large magnets fitted to cranes at a scrapyard can separate iron and steel from non-magnetic materials.

AUGMENTED REALITY

See how reactive the metals from Group 1 of the Periodic Table are by dropping samples of Lithium (Li), Potassium (K) and Caesium (Cs) into water. Stand back and watch what happens! Which metal is the most reactive?

⌐ A large scrapyard crane picking up scrap iron and steel.

CHEMICAL CHAOS

Substances contain atoms and molecules that are held together by chemical bonds. In a chemical reaction, the bonds are broken and new ones are formed as two or more substances react and turn into different substances. Chemical reactions do not create or destroy atoms, but rearrange them, creating different substances.

REACTANTS AND PRODUCTS

The "ingredients" used in a chemical reaction are called reactants. These substances change during the chemical reaction and become the "products" of a reaction. Plants make food in a chemical reaction called photosynthesis. The reactants are carbon dioxide from the air and water from the plant's roots. Using energy from sunlight, they react to create glucose (the plant's food) and oxygen.

Fireworks are fast, exothermic chemical reactions that create bright, colourful light.

The leaves of an African water lily grow to an amazing size. Thanks to photosynthesis, they can grow to more than 2m across in a single year.

FAST AND SLOW

Some reactions, such as explosions, are instant. Others take longer, such as the corrosion of iron. Iron reacts with water and oxygen in air to form red iron oxide (rust). Many reactions go only one way and cannot be reversed but some are reversible. Nitrogen and hydrogen are used in a reversible reaction to produce ammonia. Ammonia is an important chemical used in industry and to make fertilizers.

Rust is the product of the slow, corrosive chemical reaction of iron with water and oxygen.

HEAT IN

Some reactions are endothermic – they take in heat from their surroundings in order to break the chemical bonds between molecules. Instant cold packs used to treat injuries provide an example of an endothermic reaction. When a pack is activated, a barrier between the water and ammonium chloride inside the pack is broken and the two substances react, drawing heat from outside, making the pack surface ice-cold.

The chemical reaction in an instant cold pack is endothermic - it takes in heat from its surroundings.

HEAT OUT

Some reactions are exothermic – they give out heat. When chemical bonds are formed, energy is released, usually in the form of heat or light. The reactions of Group I metals with water and fluorine are exothermic reactions, as are combustion reactions in which a fuel reacts with oxygen and heat energy to burn.

When the metal powder thermite is burned it instantly generates temperatures as high as 2,400°C.

DID YOU KNOW?

Margarine is made using the metal nickel as a catalyst. The nickel helps speed up the reaction that turns vegetable oils and hydrogen into a solid that can be spread.

SPEED IT UP!

A catalyst alters the rate of a chemical reaction while remaining unchanged itself. Most catalysts speed up the rate of reaction. Metals like platinum and palladium are used inside catalytic converters in cars to speed up the conversion of harmful substances such as nitrous oxides into harmless oxygen and nitrogen. Hydrogen peroxide normally reacts very slowly, breaking down into the products oxygen and water. When potassium iodide is added as a catalyst, the reaction speeds up sharply. If a little liquid soap is also added, the oxygen and water generated by the reaction create a sudden surge of thick foam.

Adding hydrogen peroxide, potassium iodide and liquid soap together generates thick foam that looks like giant toothpaste!

ACIDS AND BASES

Acids are substances that release hydrogen ions when dissolved in water. These ions are hydrogen atoms that have lost their only electron and so have a positive electrical charge. The greater the concentration of hydrogen ions, the more acidic a substance is. Bases are the chemical opposite of acids and have a negative charge. Acids and bases react together, often in useful ways.

AMAZING ACIDS

Acids are all around you and inside you – your stomach secretes 1–3 litres of gastric juice a day containing strong hydrochloric acid which helps break down food. Edible acids such as citric acid are found in many fruits and acetic acid gives vinegar its sour taste. Carbonic acid causes limestone to dissolve and form stalactites and stalagmites in caves. Citric acid is a component of many household cleaning liquids while other acids are used to produce dyes, paints and fertilizers.

Rainwater and groundwater pick up carbon dioxide in the air to form carbonic acid. This dissolves limestone rock, which over many years can form spectacular stalactites and stalagmites in caves.

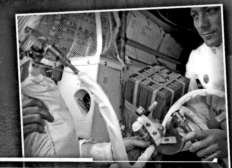

In space, the base lithium hydroxide is used to help remove carbon dioxide breathed out by astronauts from the air. It prevents dangerous levels of the gas forming in a confined space.

BRILLIANT BASES

Bases tend to feel slippery and taste bitter. They are good at breaking down fats and grease so are found in many detergents and cleaners. A base that dissolves in water is called an alkali. Both acids and bases can let electricity pass through them and are used in batteries. Longer-life alkaline batteries frequently use the base potassium hydroxide.

DANGER, DANGER!

Strong acids can dissolve many other materials and are said to be highly corrosive. Hydrofluoric acid, for instance, is stored in plastic bottles because it can eat through metal and glass. It's not just acids that can be harmful. Strong alkalis like sodium hydroxide (also known as caustic soda) can dissolve tough wood fibres in paper-making and even strip a skeleton's bones of flesh.

Nitric acid is a strong acid that can dissolve a metal coin in seconds.

ON THE SCALE

The "power of hydrogen" or pH scale measures whether something is an acid or base. The scale runs from 0 to 14 with a pH of 7 meaning a substance is neutral – neither an acid nor a base. Each number smaller on the pH scale means a substance has ten times more hydrogen ions. So, battery acid with a pH of 0 has 1,000 times more hydrogen ions than vinegar (which has a pH of 3) and one million times more acidic than saliva which has a pH of 6.

Acidic

0
1
2
3
4
5
6

Neutral 7

Alkaline (basic)

8
9
10
11
12
13

Lemon

Blood

Seawater

Bleach

ACID OR BASE?

Litmus paper is used to test the pH of liquids. When dipped in an acid the paper turns red, but in a base the litmus paper turns blue. Universal indicator can show a range of colours from red for strong acids to dark purple for strong bases with green for pH 7 (neutral).

Bee stings are acidic while wasp stings are alkaline (basic). They require different substances to neutralize them and reduce the swelling.

NEUTRALIZATION

An acid and a base can react with each other, creating neutral water and a salt. An indigestion tablet contains a base such as magnesium hydroxide, which neutralizes stomach acids that cause indigestion.

FREAKY FORCES

Forces are pushes and pulls that act on objects. They are constantly occurring all around you, often without you knowing. All forces have speed and direction and are measured in newtons (N). Some forces act over long distances, such as a planet's force of gravity on a moon. A force can change an object's speed or direction of movement or deform the object's shape.

THE FORCE OF GRAVITY

Gravity is a force of attraction between two objects. It occurs to all objects but we can only see its effects on objects with great mass such as a planet, like Earth, which pulls objects towards its centre. The Sun has so much mass (over 99.5 per cent of all the mass of the Solar System) that it exerts enough gravity to hold the planet Neptune in orbit around it, even though Neptune, at its furthest, is 4.54 billion km away.

This weightlifter needs to pull with about 1,500N of force to overcome gravity and lift a set of 150kg weights.

Like a parachute, a plane experiences drag as air pushes against it. For a plane to move forward, the force of thrust from its engine must overcome drag.

AIR RESISTANCE

A lot of the time, more than one force is at work on an object. When a parachutist jumps, the force of gravity pulls him or her towards the ground. At the same time, the force of air resistance or drag (air pushing against a moving object) acts on the skydiver to slow their fall down so they can descend safely to the ground.

AUGMENTED REALITY

Enter a Gravity Space Lab! Swipe the objects to see how the varying amounts of gravity on the Earth, on the Moon and in Space affect how they move and fall. How do things move in Space, where there is very little gravitational force?

UNDER PRESSURE

Pressure is the amount of force acting on a set area and is measured in pascals. It varies with the amount of force and the size of the area it is applied to. A drawing pin concentrates the force of your thumb pressing with low pressure on the large area of the disc into high pressure at the small area of the point. The high pressure at the point means that it can push into wood easily.

← Underwater, pressure increases with depth. In 2012, the submersible Deepsea Challenger reached the deepest part of the Pacific Ocean. It was built to withstand 1,090 times more pressure than you would find at the ocean's surface.

A nutcracker increases the force of a hand pressing on a nut's hard shell by around 4–5 times.

WORK AND MACHINES

Work is done whenever a force is applied. It is measured in joules (J) with one joule of work completed when a force of 1N is applied over a distance of 1m. A person sprinting uses about 1,000 joules per second. Machines are used to make work easier. They can do this using pulleys which can increase the lifting force of a crane. Or they use levers like those of a nutcracker. A lever consists of a beam or rod pivoted at a fixed hinge and can amplify (make bigger) the amount of force applied.

BALANCED FORCES

Sometimes, the forces acting on an object are equal and balance each other out. A helicopter pilot, for instance, can control the speed and amount of lift generated by a helicopter's rotor blades to balance out gravity, so the helicopter can hover in mid-air.

← Boats and other objects float because the force of their weight pushing down and the thrust of the water pushing up are balanced.

ON THE MOVE

Scientists define motion as a change in location or position of an object over time. The speed of an object is the time it takes to cover a certain distance. These can vary greatly. For instance, a snail's top speed is just 0.004km per hour (1mm per second) while the fastest ever jet aircraft can reach 3,530km per hour.

VELOCITY AND ACCELERATION

Velocity is the speed of an object in a particular direction. It changes if an object's speed or direction of movement alters. Acceleration is a change in velocity over time and is measured in metres (or kilometres) per second per second. When a car or bus starts off by moving slowly but then travels a greater distance in the same amount of time, it is said to accelerate.

The cheetah, the world's fastest land animal, can accelerate in short bursts of up to 30,000m per second per second.

INERTIA

Objects resist any change in their movement. If they are not moving, they continue to stay still until a force is applied. If they are moving, then they continue to move at the same speed and direction until a force acts on them. This principle is called inertia. An object with large mass such as a big truck or an elephant needs more force to overcome its inertia than something with much less mass like a bicycle or a mouse.

Inertia is the force that keeps thrill seekers pressed into their seats as a rollercoaster carriage turns upside down.

When a racing car brakes, friction is created between the wheel and the brake pad, making the brake pad reach a temperature of 1,000°C.

FRICTION

Friction is the force that resists movement when two surfaces rub together. Friction acts in the opposite direction to movement, slowing objects down and generating heat. When striking a match across a matchbox, friction generates enough heat to light the chemicals in a match head. Friction also accounts for grip; it prevents tyres and shoes from slipping on a surface.

ACTION-REACTION

When a force acts on an object, the object exerts an equal force in the opposite direction. This is called the action-reaction principle or Newton's Third Law. This principle is exhibited in the water-propelled jet pack shown here (left). A 10m hose sucks in water, which a jet-propulsion system pushes out of two nozzles, on either side of the rider. The force of the water being pushed down creates a reaction force that powers the jet pack upwards, allowing the rider to fly.

REDUCING DRAG AND FRICTION

Reducing friction helps things move faster and allows objects to use less energy. Many moving parts of machines are lubricated – covered with a thin slippery layer of liquid such as oil – in order to reduce the friction between surfaces. Drag is friction between molecules of air and a moving surface. The faster an object moves through the air, the more drag it encounters. This is why fast vehicles are built to be as streamlined as possible to let air travel around them smoothly and reduce air resistance.

Cyclists wear streamlined "skinsuits" and helmets to reduce the amount of drag acting against them.

ENERGY IN ACTION

Energy is the ability to perform work. It can never be destroyed, but it can be transferred from one object to another such as when a footballer kicks a ball or when a catapult hurls a rock. Energy comes in many different forms and can be changed from one type to another.

A solid steel wrecking ball may weigh more than 5,000kg. Swinging it on a chain increases its kinetic energy, giving it enough force to smash concrete.

CHEMICAL AND KINETIC ENERGY

Chemical energy is stored in substances such as food, coal or oil, which all rely on chemical reactions to release their energy. A battery is a store of chemical energy that can be converted into electricity when connected to a circuit (see "Switch it On"). Moving and vibrating objects have kinetic energy. An object with greater mass and greater speed has more kinetic energy.

Gravity pulls a bungee jumper towards Earth, only for energy stored in the elastic bungee rope to pull the jumper up.

LOTS OF POTENTIAL

Potential energy is energy stored in an object. A coiled spring has potential energy, which is released when the spring unwinds. When an archer fires an arrow, the potential energy of the bent bow is transferred to the arrow when it is released, becoming kinetic energy that moves the arrow. When an object is above the Earth's surface it has gravitational potential energy in the form of gravity pulling it towards the ground, giving it kinetic energy.

AUGMENTED REALITY

Now you have the force of a wrecking ball in your hands! Can you unleash its potential and kinetic energy to knock down a wall? Touch the side panel buttons to change the length of the chain, angle of the ball's swing (by adjusting the sliders) and the size of the ball (by pinching and zooming the ball). Watch what happens!

CHANGING ENERGY

Energy can be converted from one type to another. A motorbike converts the potential chemical energy from its fuel by burning it in its engine. The gases produced move the engine's pistons, turning chemical energy into kinetic energy. Food contains stores of chemical energy. The muscles in our bodies turn this into kinetic energy that allows us to move.

A racing cyclist eats a snack to give him energy. The food's chemical energy is turned into kinetic energy.

HEATING UP

The energy of molecules moving is heat. We measure the speed at which they move as temperature. Heat can flow from an area of higher temperature to one of lower temperature in different ways. In conduction heat travels through a solid as particles vibrate. Convection is the transfer of heat through a gas or liquid. Warmer gas or liquid rises while cooler liquid or gas falls. In radiation, heat moves in electromagnetic waves – such as heat moving from the Sun.

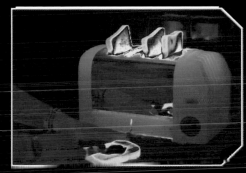

➤ In this thermogram, temperatures are measured by detecting infrared radiation. The heat of the toast (red) contrasts with the cold of the toaster (blue).

ELECTROMAGNETIC SPECTRUM

Light is a type of energy that travels in waves. Other types of wave include radio waves, microwaves, X rays, gamma rays, ultraviolet rays and infrared rays. Together they form the electromagnetic spectrum. They range from gamma rays with the shortest wavelength to radio waves with the longest.

➤ X-rays can travel through certain materials so you can see what lies underneath. They are used in medicine, airport security and also engineering.

LIGHT AND COLOUR

Visible light is made up of electromagnetic waves that travel astonishingly fast – 299,792km in a second! It takes light from the Sun a little over 8 minutes to reach us on Earth. Common sources of visible light are the Sun, light bulbs and also chemical reactions such as combustion.

LET THERE BE LIGHT

Transparent materials such as glass, air or water let light through, while opaque materials like wood and metal do not. Translucent materials, like tissue paper, let some but not all light through. When light hits an opaque object, it can either be absorbed or reflected. A rough surface tends to bounce light rays off at different angles, scattering the light, while a smooth, flat object, like a mirror, reflects light straight back.

SPLITTING COLOUR

Visible light is made up of light of different colours, with different wavelengths. Violet has the shortest wavelength and red the longest. The different colours can be split by passing light through a glass prism. When light strikes a coloured object, the object absorbs the other colours, but reflects the colour of the object back to your eyes.

Light passes through this prism and is split into all the colours of the light spectrum.

BENDING LIGHT

Light travels fast through air but a little slower through water and glass. Refraction occurs where light bends as a result of the change in speed as it passes from one medium to another. Most rainbows occur when light from the Sun strikes water in the air from rain or fog. The light is bent as it passes in and out of the water droplets, separating out the different wavelengths to form the rainbow's colours.

The straw in this glass looks broken due to the refraction of light at the point where it emerges from the water and into the air above it.

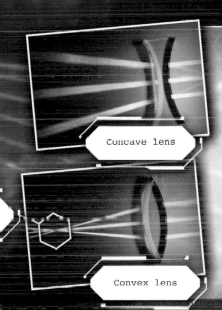

The powerful beams of lasers are used to make spectacular light shows.

Concave lens

Focal point

Convex lens

LENSES

Lenses are made of a transparent material. Light waves striking the curved, polished surface of a lens are refracted, changing direction. Concave lenses have thin centres and thicker edges. They are often used to correct the eyesight of people who are short-sighted. Convex lenses have thick centres and thinner edges which force light passing through to converge or come together at a point behind the lens called the focal point. Convex lenses are used in microscopes, telescopes and cameras to magnify objects.

DID YOU KNOW?

Some powerful telescopes are sent into space so that they can get a clear view of the stars and planets 24 hours a day. The James Webb Space Telescope to be launched in 2018 will be so powerful that it could spot a soccer ball 550km away.

LASERS

Lasers are devices that generate a wavelength of light that is concentrated in a very narrow beam. Laser light doesn't spread out as it travels so it can be used to measure long distances accurately to a fraction of a millimetre. Many lasers are used in industry to weld and shape metals and can even cut diamonds, while others are used to perform precise surgery on the human body.

A laser cutting through metal.

SOUND IT OUT

Sound is a type of energy that travels in the form of waves. These gradually lose their energy as they travel away from their source. Some materials absorb sound waves, while others reflect them, causing them to bounce back, creating an echo.

HIGH AND LOW FREQUENCY

Frequency is the speed at which a wave vibrates. It is measured in hertz (Hz) – the number of vibrations made in one second. The greater the frequency, the more vibrations in a second and the higher the pitch of the sound. Humans can hear a wide range of sounds (approximately 20–20,000Hz) but some animals such as mice, dogs and bats can hear far higher-pitched sounds.

Sound frequencies can be captured and controlled digitally on the graphic equalizers of sound systems.

Most bats can hear extremely high-pitched sounds of over 100,000Hz.

SUPERSONIC

The speed at which sound travels depends on what it's travelling through. Sound travels faster through the densely packed particles in a solid like wood than it does through a gas like air where the particles are more spaced apart. At sea level, the speed of sound through air is approximately 1,225km per hour, but is around 4.3 times faster through water. Supersonic objects are those that travel faster than the speed of sound through air.

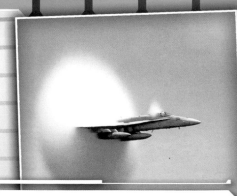

Sometimes a cloud forms as a supersonic aircraft begins to fly faster than the speed of sound, due to a decrease in air pressure.

AMPLITUDE

Amplitude is how much energy a sound has. The greater the energy, the bigger the peaks in the sound wave and the louder the sound. The loudness of a sound can be measured using the decibel (db) scale. Each jump of 10db equals a sound 10 times louder. So, an electric drill at 90db is 10 times louder than an 80db vacuum cleaner. At the quiet end of the scale are rustling leaves (20db) while gunshots can reach 140–150db, potentially damaging your hearing.

An Ariane 5 space rocket can generate sounds up to 180db as it lifts off.

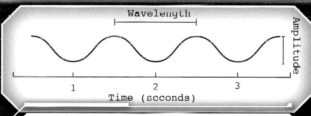

A diagram showing how the amplitude of a wave is its maximum distance from its rest position.

GOING ELECTRIC

Sounds can be captured and converted into electric signals using devices like microphones. They can then be amplified (made louder), recorded or played through loudspeakers. In digital sound recording, the electrical signals representing sound are turned into a stream of data, which can be stored on a computer as a sound file.

A microphone converts sound waves into electrical signals that can then be amplified.

GOOD VIBRATIONS

Musical instruments generate sound vibrations in different ways. Strumming a guitar creates sound waves from the strings vibrating in the air, while blowing into a saxophone, clarinet or harmonica causes a thin reed to vibrate, creating sound waves. Tightening a guitar, violin or cello string causes it to vibrate faster, generating higher pitched notes.

The strings of a guitar are tightened to different tensions so they can play at different pitches.

AUGMENTED REALITY

Get ready to explore the energy of sound! Record your voice by tapping the red button, then play it back to hear a demonstration of what can happen if you amplify the sound and change the frequency (pitch). Shout loudly and clap your hands. See if you make the glass shatter!

SHOCKING ELECTRICITY

Electricity is a natural phenomenon that people have harnessed to power the modern world. It occurs when electrons are free to jump from one atom to another while the nucleus of the atom remains in place. Electricity occurs in the natural world, including inside your body as small signals sent by nerve cells, and can be generated by technology to power all sorts of things from mobile phones to entire cars.

STATIC ELECTRICITY

All materials consist of positive and negative charges which are normally balanced out in atoms. Rubbing some objects can cause them to build up a positive or negative electric charge known as static electricity. When a balloon is rubbed on hair, electrons move from the hair to build up on the surface of the balloon, which becomes negatively charged. Because opposite charges attract, the balloon can pull the positively charged hair upwards.

ELECTRIC LIGHT

Electricity is capable of being transformed into other types of energy. An electric light bulb converts electrical energy to heat and light by heating a filament so that it glows white-hot.

The static charge from the ball causes your hair to stand on end.

HAIR-RAISING STUFF

Invented by US physicist Robert Jemison Van de Graaff, a Van de Graaff generator produces a large charge of static electricity which it transfers to a ball or dome. When you place your hand on the dome, the static charge runs through your body to your hair, making it stand on end.

LIGHTNING STRIKE!

Lightning is caused by static electricity building up in storm clouds as water droplets and ice crystals rub against each other. Large positive charges build up at the top of a cloud and negative charges at its base. Lightning occurs when these massive charges move to balance themselves out either within the clouds (sheet lightning) or towards the ground (forked lightning).

PLASMA GLOBE

A plasma globe is a clear orb filled with a mixture of unreactive noble gases and with a metal ball at the centre. When the ball is charged at high voltage the electricity acts on the gas to produce thin filaments or threads of highly energized matter known as plasma. When you place your finger on the ball, energy flows towards your finger, dragging the filaments to that point on the globe.

AUGMENTED REALITY

Experiment with static electricity with an amazing plasma globe! Flow the noble gases Neon (Ne), Argon (Ar) and Xenon (Xe) inside the globe and place your hand on the ball to set off different-coloured electrical charges. Place one finger first, then see what happens when you add other fingers.

CONDUCTORS AND INSULATORS

Materials that let electric current flow through them freely are known as electrical conductors. Many metals, like silver and copper are excellent conductors. Glass, wood, rubber and most plastics do not let their electrons flow freely and are known as insulators.

❨ Plastic insulataion covers the copper wires through which electricity flows. This makes them safe to use.

CURRENT ELECTRICITY

Electricity can also travel as a flow of electric charge, which is called an electric current. For current to flow, it needs a continuous pathway or loop known as a circuit. Electrical current can be direct and flow in one constant direction like that from a battery, or it can be alternating current like the mains electricity in your home which switches direction many times per second.

⌐It's strange but true: it's possible to produce an electric current between two halves of a lemon. The acid in the lemon acts as a great conductor of electricity.

SWITCH IT ON!

Every time you switch on a computer or turn your bedroom light on, you are channelling electricity through a circuit. Electricity travels as a flow of electrons from the power source, such as a battery. The power source produces electrical pressure, known as voltage, which pushes electrons along the wires.

CIRCUIT COMPONENTS

A circuit needs a source of power and wires to connect its various components to the power source. It must be a complete circuit, returning to the power source at the end. The simplest electrical component is a switch, such as a light switch, which you can switch off to stop the current flowing. A resistor is a component that is able to limit the flow of current in a circuit. It helps to protect other components from too much current and is used to control time delays.

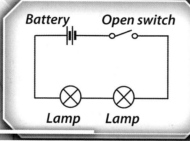

Battery *Open switch*

Lamp *Lamp*

A circuit diagram represents a circuit using symbols. This one shows two lamps connected in a series to a battery, with a switch.

SERIES AND PARALLEL CIRCUITS

In a series circuit, the current flows through every component in turn. If one component doesn't work, such as one bulb in a set of fairy lights, then the entire circuit will fail. In a parallel circuit, the electricity is shared between several paths. If one part fails, the rest can still operate. The lighting in most buildings is on a parallel circuit so that if one part stops working, the rest can still operate.

Many fairy lights run on a series circuit, sharing just one main electrical path.